How To
BUILD
Your Network Marketing
NUTRITION
Business
FAST

KEITH & TOM "BIG AL" SCHREITER

How To Build Your Network Marketing Nutrition Business Fast

© 2020 by Keith & Tom "Big Al" Schreiter

Published by Fortune Network Publishing

PO Box 890084

Houston, TX 77289 USA

Telephone: +1 (281) 280-9800

BigAlBooks.com

ISBN-13: 978-1-948197-63-2

CONTENTS

I travel the world 240+ days each year.
Let me know if you want me to stop in your
area and conduct a live Big Al training.

BigAlSeminars.com

FREE Big Al Training Audios
Magic Words for Prospecting
plus Free eBook and the Big Al Report!

BigAlBooks.com/free

PREFACE

Do we sell health and wellness nutritional products?

If we market products to improve health, this book will be a treasure trove of ideas on how to get our prospects to become customers or distributors.

Not every idea here will be the perfect idea for the perfect situation. But all it takes is one good idea to change our business and our income forever.

In this book we will cover great things to say and do for our products and for our opportunities. Remember, it is the quality, rather than the quantity, of ideas that we learn that makes the difference. And we have to put them into action.

Health products are "preventative" and difficult to market to new prospects. Why? Because they may not see or feel an immediate difference.

There is an old saying, "Selling prevention is difficult. Selling a cure is easy."

Prospects will eagerly take action for a cure. Here is an example.

We get a notice from our dentist that our annual checkup is approaching. We don't feel motivated.

But then we get a toothache. We take instant action and call for an appointment.

In most countries, health products are classified as prevention. Pharmaceutical drugs are classified as cures.

But don't worry. We can learn great things to say and do to market our health products. That is why having the right words makes a difference.

Please note, many states, countries, and health agencies have varying laws. And of course, our companies have a variety of guidelines also. Because what we can and cannot say changes frequently, check the current rules for health claims and advice with your company.

But all the examples in this books will help us create better words that get results. Our words can help more people take advantage of what we offer.

Let's get started right away with some great things to say and do.

Decisions.

We are in the "decision-making" business. Our company provides the products, the website, the lawyers, the customer service departments, and will even ship directly to our customers.

In fact, our company can do everything except …

Get prospects to make "yes" decisions to become customers, or to join as distributors.

And that is why our company needs us.

The company does almost everything. All we have to do is get "yes" decisions from our prospects.

Wow! This is a great deal for us. Why?

Because our job is easy. Once we learn how prospects make decisions, we can build a huge business in record time. Getting new customers? Easy. Getting new team members? No problem.

So the obvious question is, "How do prospects make decisions?"

Well, the answer might surprise us.

So, let's get down to business.

This is not how people make decisions:

- They wait for the universe to give them a sign.
- They listen to the little whispers in their heads.
- 10,000 reasons for, and 9,000 reasons against.

- They sit through an hour-long presentation, watch videos and look at PowerPoint slides, listen to testimonials, and at the end of the presentation, they carefully weigh the pros and cons, and then make a logical decision based upon the facts.

Well, this might be what others have taught us, but the reality is much different.

If we knew exactly how humans made up their minds, how much would that be worth to us?

Millions.

And that is why we should continue reading.

Here is the short story.

The science of decision-making is an enormous subject. We won't go there in this book.

All we need to learn are four simple steps to get our prospects to make a "yes" decision, so we have a successful network marketing health products business.

Step #1. Build rapport. If our prospects don't trust us or like us, then nothing we can present will make much difference. Thankfully, we only have to spend a few seconds on this step to get the trust and belief we need.

Step #2. Ice breaker. Now that our prospects will listen to us, we can introduce our business into a social conversation. Many times our prospects will make their final "yes" decision here, based on how we describe our business. Our prospects might think, "Yeah, that sounds good. I want that."

Step #3. Closing. After we give our prospects a brief hint about our business in our ice breaker, they will have some pre-existing programs in their minds. They could have a program that means they want to live longer. They could have a program that they deserve to earn more money. For these prospects, a "yes" decision is instant. And for others, we can prompt them to make a "yes" or "no" decision with just a phrase or two.

The above three steps might take 15 seconds. Relax. It is hard to believe now, but we will see how it works in this book.

Step #4. If the answer to Step #3 is "yes," then and only then will we give a presentation.

And that is it. Our presentation could take as little as 15 seconds, or as long as our prospects want. In this book we will cover many mini-presentations that only take a few sentences.

Now, back to the short story.

We will learn these four little steps, and we will get "yes" decisions.

So get ready for more customers and team members.

But first, we need to find people to talk to.

Who can I talk to first?

Before we can follow the four conversation steps, we first need someone to talk to. So how do we get an appointment to talk to others?

Let's take a look at the three types of prospects.

First, our relatives and close friends.

There is an old saying, "Dogs know who to bite."

The people who know us best will be able to tell when we're trying to sell them something. They sense desperation and an agenda. If they are going to sense our agenda, what should our agenda be?

To try to help them.

Before we talk to our close relatives and friends, let's think about our agenda. What is an agenda? It is our thoughts and intentions for the expected outcome.

Prospects notice our tone of voice, our micro-facial expressions, and our body language. Whatever our chosen agenda, it will shine through. Our agenda will have more impact than the actual words we say.

Before we say our first words, let's establish our agenda in our minds. We should think:

1. I want to help them.

2. I will offer an "option."

3. They can decide if this option works for them or not.

And what will this option be?

Maybe we will offer them an opportunity to have a second income in their lives, to build a better immune system, or to take care of their bodies so they live longer.

But remember, we are offering an option. That means no convincing, and no high-pressure sales techniques.

Think of it like picking a restaurant to go to. We can suggest a restaurant to our close relatives and friends, but it is okay if they choose not to go there.

Our prospects appreciate extra options in their lives. Who wouldn't? We could say, "This is one more option for your life. You can take advantage of this option now, later, or never. But you will always have this extra option."

This means no rejection and no pressure. We give our prospects an option. Done.

Our relatives and close friends know us well. They will instantly detect our intention.

What to say to relatives and close friends.

We have rapport and trust with these people. They have experience with us. However, we will feel guilty if they think we are just trying to make money off them. Having "options" as our agenda will help us avoid that.

Still, we might feel hesitant to approach everyone that we know. And some people are intimidating. We have no idea how to approach them without rejection.

To solve this, we will use the comfortable/uncomfortable formula. This allows us to tell them we have an opportunity, but gives them an escape so they don't feel trapped. Here it is in action.

"Mary, I am perfectly comfortable with your decision to look at my business or not. But I was uncomfortable not asking if you wanted to look, and having you think that I didn't care."

How does Mary feel when she hears this invitation to learn about our business? If she has an interest, she feels honored that we wanted to talk to her right away. If she doesn't have an interest, we told her that it is okay if she doesn't want to look at our business. She doesn't feel bad. We didn't jeopardize our friendship, so we don't feel guilty. And with this formula, we can approach everyone.

Let's do another example.

"David, I am listening to an online business presentation tonight. This is a business that you can do too. I am comfortable if you want to join me tonight, or not. No problem. I don't even know what you have scheduled. But I just felt uncomfortable not letting you know about this business."

How does David feel? Good. He has options. We don't judge him or our friendship based on which option he takes.

Another example?

"Hi, Laura. I got tired of working two jobs for extra money, so I started a part-time business out of my home. I thought it might be interesting for you also. I am comfortable if you want to take a look at it, or not. I just felt uncomfortable not letting you know about it."

With this comfortable/uncomfortable technique, we only take the volunteers.

The volunteers are ready for action. If we press for an appointment, what does that signal? Either our prospects are skeptical of our approach, or it is not the right time for them. Both situations will waste everyone's time and make everyone feel bad. But if we use this technique to get to the point quickly, we can sort out who is interested and who isn't and still maintain our friendships.

We can do the same kind of invitation for customers. Here is a quick example.

"Hey Peter. We are both getting older and don't have the energy we had at 16 years old. So I am drinking a special breakfast drink to help me feel younger, so I can keep up with my teenagers. I am okay if you want to try this breakfast drink or not, but I at least wanted to let you know what I am doing. I didn't want you to feel like I wouldn't think of you right away."

As we can see, if we don't like using comfortable/uncomfortable, we could adjust. In this case we used the word "okay" instead, but we get the general idea.

Second group? People we know who are not relatives or close friends.

We may not have rapport with these people. So we will have to do a bit more work to connect with them. These people will want a good reason to meet with us. And this means they will want to protect themselves from salespeople and time-consuming presentations.

We have two ways to get them interested in meeting with us.

First way: We can tell them we have wonderful benefits.

Let's list a few of these benefits now:

- Feel younger.

- Live longer.

- Help their children's immune system.

- Fewer doctor appointments.

- A second income to pay their bills.

- A chance to work from home instead of going to work.

We could simply ask them if one of these benefits interests them. For example, "Would you like to have energy all afternoon instead of doing all that yawning?"

It won't take long for them to say, "Sure. Let's talk." Or, they could also say, "No thanks. I feel better when I suffer and struggle all afternoon. Please don't help me."

Why would they want to suffer and avoid a solution from us? We don't know. But here are a few reasons they wouldn't want to continue this conversation:

- They had a bad experience with a pushy salesman last week.

- We look like their ex-girlfriend or ex-boyfriend. Nothing we can do about that.

- We said the wrong words.

- They believe health comes from a diet soda.

- Their minds are on something else right now.

- We have bad breath.

So don't worry. This is life. Some want to improve their lives, some don't.

The good news is this choice is over in seconds. And because we gave them a choice, no one is offended.

Second way: We can let them know we might have a solution to their problems.

This is even more powerful. We worry about our problems all the time. Here are a few problems they might have:

- Low energy.
- Challenged immune system.
- Their kids don't like healthy food.
- Growing old.
- Meager retirement savings.
- A time-consuming commute to work.
- A terrible boss or soul-sucking career.

In this case our conversation would look like this:

Us: "Do you have [this problem]? Would it be okay if we could fix it?"

Here are a few examples:

Us: "Do you hate working here at the shopping mall on Saturdays?"

Prospect: "Of course."

That was easy. Here is the second example.

Us: "Would it be okay if there was another option?"

Prospect: "Sure. When can we talk?"

That was easy. Here is a third example.

Us: "Do you find growing old really hurts?"

Prospect: "Yes! Every little task is harder too."

Us: "Would it be okay if we tried some natural ways to slow down the aging process?"

Prospect: "Sure. When can we talk?"

Third group? People we don't know at all.

Now conversations get harder with this group. When they first come into contact with us, they will be thinking:

- Who is this person?
- What does this person want?
- Can I trust this person?
- Should I set up my salesmen defenses?
- Is it time to be skeptical?
- Should I hide my wallet?
- Try to avoid a time-wasting sales pitch.

These thoughts mean we don't have rapport with this stranger.

We will spend time attempting to get trust and rapport. Once we accomplish this, then we can move on to getting an appointment. Yes, it might take two or more engagements with a stranger to create rapport first.

Some people are natural trust-builders. They can achieve rapport in seconds. Other people? We have to work harder to connect with strangers.

A few words to disable strangers' fear.

Here is a quick example of how easy it can be to help strangers relax and feel more comfortable.

If our stranger puts up a wall of defenses and mistrust, we can immediately say:

"Relax, you don't have to do anything, and things will remain the same. But if you want a way to work out of your home instead of commuting to work, I can let you know about one option now."

That sounds pretty non-threatening.

Next, let's learn a few ways to soothe our own anxiety about talking to prospects.

How to fix "feeling nervous" when talking to prospects.

It isn't our presentation that makes us nervous; it's our intention.

Is our intention to sign them up or get them to buy our products?

Well, that will show in everything we say and do. Prospects can smell aggressive salespeople a mile away.

But what if we only intend to offer them an **option**? We don't care if they take the option or not, we only care that they know they have the option.

Then we neutralize our personal feelings and accept whatever decision our prospects make. We want what is best for them. And then what happens? Our prospects will pick up on our new intention and relax. Now our conversations become stress-free.

Maybe we could start by saying, "Would you like to hear an option?"

And if they say "yes," then our conversation will be easy and enjoyable.

An option means, "It is okay if you take advantage of this or not. No one is going to pressure you either way." This feels very safe for prospects. They relax, and they have no reason to reject us.

To avoid feeling nervous, simply remember the word, "option."

But it gets better!

Here is the best news of all.

Most people are pre-sold on what we have to offer. That means we don't have to sell.

No selling. If our prospects already want what we have, all we have to do is avoid talking them out of it.

If this seems hard to believe, let's take a survey. We will go out and ask 50 people, "Do you want to live longer, or die quickly?" Almost everyone wants to live longer. They might smile at this statement, but they definitely want to live longer and are pre-sold.

Next, we will ask 50 people, "Do you want more money in your life, or less money?" Most people want extra money. They want to hear more from us.

Wow!

So here is our new approach.

1. Prospects want what we have to offer.

2. Don't be a pushy salesman and try to convince them.

3. Instead, give them the option of our products and opportunity.

4. Let them choose if now is a good time for them to say "yes."

That wasn't so hard, was it?

No more fear of talking to prospects. All we do is gift them with one more option in their lives. Gifting is fun.

Now, let's move on to the four steps of conversation we will use when we talk to our prospects. Remember them?

Step #1: Rapport.

Step #2: Ice breaker.

Step #3: Closing.

Step #4: Presentation.

Step #1:
Build rapport first.

Rapport means that our prospects trust us and believe us. If they don't, they won't buy or join.

Rapport is different from relationships. We can create trust and belief in a few seconds. Relationships? Well, those take a lot longer. We don't have to worry about deep relationship-building now. All we have to do is to create enough trust and belief to deliver our message.

This decision to trust and believe only takes seconds.

Prospects prejudge us harshly in the first few seconds. Humans make quick decisions. Why?

Thousands of years ago, a caveman would meet a stranger. He had to make a quick decision. Will this stranger be helpful? Or will this stranger be dangerous? If the caveman spent too much time thinking it over, it could have proved fatal.

What about today? When a stranger walks through the door, we instantly prejudge the stranger. Will it be okay if the stranger sits next to me? Should I guard my wallet or purse? Why is this stranger wearing a mask and carrying an axe? Yes, we still make snap decisions based upon a few seconds' worth of information.

Our first challenge in network marketing is to build good rapport with our prospects.

But first, some good news. We already have rapport with most of the people we know. Unless we stole their car or got them fired, most people will trust and believe what we say.

But we don't have rapport with strangers. We will have to be conscious in our efforts to build rapport with them, but it will only take a few seconds.

The first few seconds we invest in building rapport are the most important part of our conversation. We have to have rapport before we deliver our message.

What happens if we don't build rapport? Our prospects will think:

- "What's the catch?"
- "I don't know you."
- "You sound like a salesman. I need to be careful."
- "What do you want from me?"
- "It's too good to be true."

When our prospects have these thoughts, they protect themselves by creating objections to keep us away. What do these objections sound like?

- "I need to talk to my spouse about it."
- "I am too busy."
- "I need to think it over."
- "It is not for me."

- "I am happy with my current situation. No new ideas, please."

Ready, set, go.

How do we build rapport in the first few seconds?

By letting people know that we think the same way they do. Prospects are more comfortable with people who are more like them than people who are different from them.

How do we emphasize our similarities?

By telling our prospects a fact that they believe and we believe. Starting with one little fact that we have in common helps create belief and trust.

We want a library of facts to choose from so we are ready for any situation with any prospect. Here are some good opening lines and facts that we can use for health products:

- Things are so stressful nowadays.
- Mornings are … difficult.
- We all want to live longer.
- It would be nice to have the energy of a 16-year-old.
- It would feel great to fall asleep within seven minutes of our heads touching the pillow.
- We have to keep our immune systems healthy.
- Our children are exposed to so many germs as soon as they go to school.
- Dying early is inconvenient. (Okay, a little dark humor.)

- One of the first symptoms of heart disease is death.
  (Okay, maybe taking the humor too far.)

These facts are safe. They also introduce our business into a social conversation. This is a great way to both be in agreement with our prospects and to move our conversation forward.

Some facts about our business opportunity?

- Commuting to work gets harder and harder.
- We would love to spend more time with our family.
- It would be great to pay for the holidays with cash instead of credit cards.
- Two paychecks are better than one.
- It is difficult to get a pay raise now.
- We wish weekends were longer.
- We dream about firing the boss.

A good way of looking at this is that starting with agreement is good manners. People like people who think like they do.

Make it better.

How?

Two facts are better than one. When we tell our prospects two true facts in a row, their brains say, "I can trust you."

Now that we have our prospects' trust, it will be easier to talk about our business. Here are some examples of putting two facts together:

- "Things are expensive now. We all need more money."
- "Of course we need good nutrition. But most healthy drinks taste like grass!"

- "Of course we should take vitamins, but we always wonder, 'Are they working?'"

- "Jobs interfere with our week. It would be nice to have three-day weekends forever."

- "It is hard to get a raise now. But, prices keep going up and up."

- "Having our own business sounds great. However, we have to be careful not to take too much risk."

All we are doing is assuring our prospects that we see the world the same way they do. This makes them feel more comfortable in dealing with us.

What happens when we start with disagreement?

Our prospects build a wall that shuts out our message. No matter how good our message or offering is, our prospects won't hear it.

We want our prospects in an open, positive state of mind. Then we can deliver our message. Once our message is inside their heads, they can decide if our message will serve them or not. That means we don't have to use any high-pressure closing techniques. All we have to do is deliver our message without a lot of baggage or prejudice.

The decision to trust us or not happens quickly.

We have to be fast. Those first few seconds make the difference. So what can we do to increase our chances of rapport?

Using certain magic words and phrases helps our prospects agree with us. Let's start with "most people."

Here is what happens when we say, "Most people."

Our prospects think, "Am I part of most people, or am I part of less people? Well, most people are part of most people, so I must be in that group. Plus I enjoy being part of most people. It feels safe. That is why I choose a crowded restaurant instead of an empty restaurant. That is why I want to walk through a dark alley late at night with a group of people instead of alone."

Notice how this feels when we say:

- "Most people hate getting sick."
- "Most people want to give their children the best nutrition before going to school."
- "Most people want more money."
- "Most people would rather work from their homes."
- "Most people want to make their lives better."

By using "most people," our phrases make it easier for prospects to trust and believe us. But this isn't the only magic phrase we could use. Let's look at the phrase, "Everybody knows." Some examples?

- "Everybody knows health is more important than money."
- "Everybody knows it will be hard to get pay raises this year."
- "Everybody knows home businesses get great tax deductions."

- "Everybody knows our bodies are made out of what we eat."

- "Everybody knows that if we work hard, only our boss gets a big house when he retires."

- "Everybody knows we don't get paid enough."

- "Everybody knows that nutrition is the secret to good health."

- "Everybody knows that if we don't do something different now, then tomorrow will be a repeat of today."

Or, we could use the phrase, "Everybody says." These words have the same effect as "everybody knows." Our prospects will want to agree with what we say. It is easier to take the path of least resistance.

A word about smiling.

Smiling works!

Our natural tendency is to trust people who smile, and to distrust people who don't smile. It doesn't take a rocket scientist to figure out that we should smile when we meet new prospects.

Babies react to smiles before they can talk. If we smile as we walk down a street, many people will smile back.

If we think being extremely serious works, we won't have many prospects buying or joining.

Remember, our prospects make their initial decision to trust and believe us within a few seconds. A smile on our faces helps them feel more comfortable with us. We want to do everything possible to keep our prospects' minds open so that they hear our good message.

And if we're not in the habit of smiling, now is the time to practice!

Do compliments work?

Direct compliments sometimes feel insincere. We make our prospects uncomfortable. Some examples of direct compliments?

- "Hi, what a beautiful home."
- "You seem like a smart consumer."
- "You are looking sharp today."

Compliments like these appear too obvious, and seem shallow.

What is a better way to give a compliment?

Focus on something a bit less obvious, and then add a question. When we add a question at the end of our compliment, our prospects don't have to acknowledge it and thank us. Instead, they focus on answering our question. This is more comfortable for everyone. Some examples?

- "I like your car. How did you go about choosing that model?"
- "I see you like eating healthy. What motivated you to eat healthy when everyone seems to be eating so much junk?"
- "Your children are so polite. How did you get them to be that way?"

So yes, compliments do work. But adding a question at the end makes everyone feel better about them.

Let's move on to introducing our business into the conversation.

Step #2:
Ice breakers.

What is the definition of an ice breaker? A short sentence that introduces our business into a social conversation in a socially-acceptable way.

We can't keep our business a secret forever. At some point we will have to let our prospects know what we're offering. We meet many prospects in social situations, and that means we should be careful about how we bring our business into our conversations.

Ever feel so excited about our business that we forget about our prospects' feelings? We want to tell our prospects everything about our business, but do they actually want to know everything? Of course not. Here is what is socially acceptable and polite.

Give our prospects an option to hear more, or to change the conversation.

Have we ever been in a situation where someone jumps into a sales presentation that we don't want to hear? They talk and talk because they are excited. We are not. It is torture.

We don't want to be that person.

Instead, our ice breaker will introduce our business. Then we will pause, giving our prospects a chance to say, "Tell me more." Or they can change the subject because they are not interested.

It is polite for us to let them decide what they want, and being polite works.

Why is this pause important? Because prospects want choices. Prospects have limited time and a lot on their minds. In the next moment, our prospects will make a decision. They will choose to know more, or they will choose to move on to the next item on their to-do list.

Here is our strategy. We will make our ice breaker so powerful that our prospects beg us for more information.

Think about this. If our prospects beg us for more information, what decision have they made? They are making a "yes" decision. This means we won't even have to close at the end of our conversation.

Our ice breaker is so important to getting that final "yes" decision. And this all happens in the first few seconds of our conversation. Closing doesn't happen at the end of our conversation. Prospects make their decision early and quickly, because they want to move on with their lives.

Rapport first.

We took the time to build rapport. Now our prospects trust and believe us. This is the perfect time to introduce our business.

But do our prospects care about us? No.

Do they care about what we have to offer? No.

Prospects care about themselves. The world revolves around them. When we introduce our business with ice breakers, we want to focus on our prospects, not on us and our business.

Our ice breakers will sound self-centered and awkward if they are about us. Some examples of bad ice breakers?

Us at a funeral, talking to the widow: "I am so sorry about your husband's death. But did you know we just introduced the only food supplement with documented Vitamin D uptake?"

Slightly exaggerated, but we get the point. We need to pay more attention to our prospects' situations.

Consider this scenario. We are at a party. Everyone at the party looks like a great prospect for us. They are enjoying life. They want to live longer. They could use an extra income. We just can't wait to talk to them, but how do we start the conversation?

Us: "What is your name?"

Prospect: "My name is Carol."

Us: "Carol. Your name starts with the letter 'C.' My company starts with the letter 'C.' Let me tell you about my company now."

Yes, this seems forced, because it was all about us. We forgot to focus on our prospects and their needs.

And did we notice that we didn't pause? We wanted to go right into our presentation. We didn't give our prospect a chance to opt out of it. That's pretty rude.

Now, let's improve our ice breaker technique.

Commanding our prospects' attention.

It is easy to get someone's attention. All we have to say is, "I just found out."

What is the other person thinking? The other person might wonder, "What did you find out? Is it something I need to know? Will this be important to me?"

Those four simple words, "I just found out," grab our prospects' attention and also give us a chance to introduce our business. Here are some examples of using these words for our ice breakers.

- "I just found out how we can feel great every time we wake up."
- "I just found out how we can lose weight without going on a diet."
- "I just found out how we can help protect our children from all those viruses and bacteria at school."
- "I just found out how we can get super nutrition, without having to eat grass and weird stuff."
- "I just found out how we can get an extra paycheck."
- "I just found out how we can work out of our homes instead of commuting to a job."
- "I just found out how we can go into business together, and do it part-time."

We can almost feel the "yes" answers after we make our "I just found out" statements. Closing feels automatic.

And we know our prospects want what we offer when they reply, "Tell me more. How does that work?"

Why does this work so well?

1. We don't set off any salesman alarms. We make a statement, and prospects can volunteer their interest by asking us to tell them more.

2. We only continue talking to prospects who are interested. They asked us for a presentation. No pressure from us.

3. This approach is 100% rejection-free. There is nothing holding us back from talking to prospects.

It feels good when we don't have to pressure our prospects, doesn't it?

Want to make this completely safe and easy?

All we have to do is continue the conversation on a different topic after we announce what we "just found out." How does this sound?

- "I just found out how we can get an extra paycheck. If you would ever like to know how, I would be glad to tell you. Meanwhile, let's ask your cousin to join us tonight at the event."

- "I just found out how we can start getting younger, instead of getting older. If you would ever like to know how, I would be glad to tell you. Meanwhile, let's go shopping."

- "I just found out how we can have more energy than our grandchildren. If you would ever like to know how, I would be glad to tell you. Meanwhile, tell me how you got this recipe."

Because we continue the conversation on a different topic, our prospects don't have to comment on our announcement. They can ask us for more details if they are interested, or ignore our ice breaker if they aren't interested.

This means we will only have conversations about our business with people who want to know more.

What happens when we try to force a discussion about our business? If our prospects don't want to hear more, they are afraid to say, "I've decided that I am not interested. And I made this decision even before I heard what it is." That would sound silly. So what do they do? They make up phantom objections. Here are some examples of phantom objections they use to keep us from continuing with a presentation.

- "I am not a salesman."
- "I don't have any time."
- "It is a pyramid."
- "This is not for me."

Prospects use these objections to protect themselves from unwanted presentations.

We won't have to worry about these objections anymore. We will only talk to the volunteers.

Ice breakers are fun.

And they are so easy to do. The first step is to make a list of our benefits. We will want benefits for our products and for our opportunity. Let's start a list right now.

Benefits for our products.

- How to live longer.

- Lose weight naturally without dieting.

- Build a killer immune system.

- Fall asleep within seven minutes of our heads touching the pillow.

- Stop rusting from the inside out.

- So much energy it would take a tranquilizer dart to bring us down.

- Wake up every morning feeling like a million dollars.

- Look younger from the inside out.

- Turns our body into a lean and mean energy machine.

- Feel like we are 16 years old again, but with better judgment.

- Great nutrition for pizza-lovers who are tired of eating rabbit food.

- Like the "Fountain of Youth" in a capsule.

Benefits for our opportunity.

- Never show up for work again.

- Work from home instead of commuting.

- Retire 10 years early at full pay.

- Double our pension in only nine months.

- Get two paychecks instead of one.

- Fire our boss.

- Work three weeks out of the month but get paid for four.
- Take a one-week holiday every month.
- Take a six-month holiday twice a year.
- Have a monthly income to pay off our student loans.
- Earn more money part-time than our boss does full-time.
- Let someone else pay for our holidays.
- A chance to send your mother-in-law a postcard from Bali.
- Pay for Christmas with cash instead of credit cards.
- Better than working 45 years like our parents.

These are some benefits to start with. All we have to do is begin our ice breaker with the words, "I just found out." Then, add an appropriate benefit for our prospects.

If our ice breaker resonates with our prospects, they will make a mental "yes" decision and ask us to tell them more.

No stress. No selling. No ugly social mistakes.

If we are observant, we can customize our benefit to fit our prospect. This is what professionals do. So take a moment to try and understand our prospect.

For example, imagine we talk to a retail clerk during the weekend. We could say, "I just found out how to never have to work weekends again." That could be a huge motivation for this retail clerk.

Another example of being observant?

While talking with a retired person we could say, "I just found out how we can stop our bodies from rusting from the inside out." Our prospect will want to know more.

Or imagine we have a conversation while waiting to pay for our groceries. The other person has a handful of coupons ready so she can save money on her purchase. Easy. We say, "I see you like to save money. I just found out how we can get an extra paycheck."

Our prospects make quick decisions based upon the words we use. This is why some networkers have all the prospects they need, while others struggle. When we say the wrong words, no one wants to volunteer. So instead of blaming prospects for being unmotivated, we should change the words we say.

Here is a little conversation that helps us remember that we influence the outcome by saying better words.

Distributor: "My prospects weren't interested."

Us: "Weren't interested in what?"

Distributor: "Weren't interested in what I said."

Us: "Then, stop blaming the prospects ... and change what you say."

It is all over in seconds.

In the first few seconds, our prospects judge us and make their decisions. That is why we have to be effective during these first few seconds.

So instead of spending hours practicing our long presentation, we should memorize great benefits that will interest our prospects. Now our job is not to convince prospects. Our job is to mention our benefits and allow prospects to volunteer.

Is "I just found out" the only opening for an ice breaker?

No.

For variety, we can use many other opening phrases. Let's look at another phrase that gets our message into a social conversation.

"Would you like to know more?"

We mention a benefit, and ask our prospects if they would like to know more. If they do, we are glad to give them more details.

This is permission-based prospecting, and it is good manners.

Being polite reduces rejection. We want to give our prospects a chance to opt out of our prospecting conversation. No one likes pushy salespeople.

What are some phrases we could use to make our prospecting conversations easier?

- "Would you like to know more?"
- "Would you like to know how I am doing it?"
- "Would you like to hear how they did it?"

Our bonus for using these phrases early in our conversations?

When prospects say they want to know more, they make a "yes" decision.

Prospects know if they want something or not.

Humans love to make "yes" or "no" decisions quickly. Then, if the answer is "yes," we welcome a presentation and more information.

Most problems arise when we push sales presentations on prospects. Avoid this grief with simple little questions, such as:

- "Would you like to know more?"
- "Would you like to know how I am doing it?"
- "Would you like to hear how they did it?"

"Why do people hate to sell?"

Because they believe selling is like what they see in the movies. In Hollywood, an actor plays the role of the aggressive, ethically-challenged salesman, who forces people to buy against their will. Okay, maybe this is what happened in the 1970s, but the 1970s are not coming back.

The old model of selling? Make cold calls. Lots of cold calls. Pitch anyone and everyone who will listen. And, if we can get an appointment, dump everything we know about our opportunity or product on the prospect. Sell, sell, sell.

After we beat our glazed-eyed prospects into submission, then we go for the close. We use trial closes, hard closes, any close that could shame our prospects into buying. And if they don't buy immediately? Then we follow up. We harass our prospects until they buy or die.

Does that sound like fun? Of course not. Nobody wants to sell that way. Yet many people today still use the old way of selling.

This is not how prospects buy anyway. It is out of sync with the buying process. Would we like to be sold this way?

This explains our reluctance to make calls, our fear of prospects, and why people don't want to join our business.

Here is the short story.

Prospects want to know the big picture first. They can immediately make a "yes" or "no" decision, based upon the current programs in their mind. If the answer is "yes," then and only then should we begin a presentation.

If this seems reasonable, that our prospects make their final decision within the first 20 seconds, then we are in sync with how our prospects love to buy. No more presentations until our prospects make a "yes" decision.

Want an example of this more humane way of talking to prospects using, "Would you like to know more?"

> **Distributor:** "I help families get an extra paycheck. Would you like to know more?"
>
> **Prospect:** "Yes. Tell me more."

Our business is simple when we don't have to hard-sell prospects. This feels right. A few mor examples:

> **Distributor:** "I am feeling 25 years younger. Would you like to know how I am doing it?"
>
> **Prospect:** "Yes. Tell me more."
>
> **Distributor:** "My blood tests got back to normal in just 6 months. Would you like to know what I did?"
>
> **Prospect:** "Yes. Tell me more."

Now, did that feel comfortable for our prospects? Comfortable for us also? Yes!

Distributor: "My neighbor is losing six pounds a month, and can still eat pizza. Would you like to know how he is doing it?"

Prospect: "Yes. Tell me more."

No one gets offended by this kind of conversation. And even if we were talking to cold prospects, they would want to know more details also.

Distributor: "I am paying off all my credit cards by the end of this year. Would you like to know how I am doing it?"

Prospect: "Yes. Tell me more."

Distributor: "My friend finally got rid of his job, and now works from home. Would you like to know how he did it?"

Prospect: "Yes. Tell me more."

Distributor: "I started a small part-time business. It only gives me 20% of my salary, but it also means I only have to work four days a week now. Would you like to know how I did it?"

Prospect: "Yes. Tell me more."

We could use this technique anywhere. Networking events. Family reunions. Idle conversations during coffee breaks at work.

This is the safest way to introduce our business to prospects. When prospects can volunteer to know more, they feel open-minded and positive about what we will say next.

Want to be a little more professional?

Yes, we can guess which benefits would help our prospects. But there is a better way.

Listen for hints.

Allow our prospects to tell us exactly the problems they have in their lives. All we have to do is sort through these problems and find one that we can help with. Now our ice breakers precisely target the problems and concerns of our prospects.

The result? We look like a mind-reader.

1. Our prospect has a problem.

2. We have a great solution.

3. We allow our prospect to decide if now is a good time to fix their problem.

An example.

Prospect: "I hate commuting downtown every day. It takes over an hour each way."

Us: "My friend, Ben, stopped commuting last year. He now works out of his home. Would you like to know how he did it?"

Prospect: "Tell me more!"

Or,

Prospect: "It is hard to work, commute, and take care of the family. So much stress every day."

Us: "I just found out how we can reduce our stress naturally. Would you like to know how others are doing it?"

Prospect: "Tell me more!"

Sometimes, this business feels so easy.

Step #3: Closing.

Step #1: We build rapport. Our prospects trust us and believe us.

Step #2: Our ice breaker creates interest. Our prospects instantly decide if they want these benefits or not.

At the end of step #2, if our prospects ask for more details, they want what we have to offer.

Will 100% of our prospects want what we have to offer immediately? No. Maybe they had a fight with their spouse 30 minutes before they talked with us. We can't control our prospects' timing. However, we can control the words we say. This gives us our best chance to get a customer or a new distributor.

A good way to look at closing is that our prospects now have a chance to take advantage of our message, or not. What a relief! We don't have to look like some pushy salesman from the movies.

At the end of step #2, our prospects have options. They could say:

- "That sounds great. Let's do it. Give me the details now." (Yes!)

- "That sounds great. I have other pending issues right now." (This is not for me right now.)

- "Did you see the game on TV last night?" (This is not for me.)

We are not in charge of our prospects' lives. They are. They must live with their decisions and the subsequent consequences. We deliver a great message, and the rest is up to them.

Some prospects might say, "I don't want to change. Let me continue on the fast track to dying early." Their choice, not our choice. Not everyone makes sensible decisions for their lives. They probably have other problems too. We don't have the psychology qualifications to deal with all of their problems.

Remember, our job is to deliver a great message. That is it.

So we just let closing ... happen?

Yes. We appreciate the same courtesy in our lives. We appreciate the option of a salesperson honoring our choices.

But don't prospects need more information to make up their minds?

Choices come first. Information comes later.

Prospects don't need information if they've made a "no" decision. That would waste their time and our time.

How long will it take prospects to decide if they want better health or not? Seconds.

How long will it take prospects to decide if they want an extra paycheck in their lives or not? Seconds.

If our prospects make a "yes" decision, then we can move forward and give them any information they want.

Seem strange? Here is an example.

At the end of a meeting, we say to the attendees, "By a show of hands, who wants to come with me to get pizza when we finish?" Most attendees will make an instant "yes" or "no" decision. Maybe half of the attendees raise their hands.

Decision made.

The decision for pizza came **before** we said where the restaurant is, what toppings are available, how much saturated fat would be in each slice, etc. Some of the attendees who raised their hands will have a few questions about this. Other attendees can't wait to leave for pizza.

It is the same process with our prospects. The simple decision to be healthier, or to have more income every month, takes about one second.

We ask our prospects to decide if they want our benefits or not. The details can come later.

No pressure.

We effectively give our prospects an escape plan. They won't feel trapped by a salesman with a single-minded agenda. Prospects relax when they feel that they are in charge of their choices, and that we are not there to argue with them.

When our prospects make their "yes" decision, how do we move forward? How do we make sure that now is the right time to proceed safely?

If we feel shy about closing, or if we want to get permission to continue, here are a few phrases that might feel comfortable:

- "Let's get that sorted."
- "Let's fix that now."

These phrases make it easy for our prospects to move forward with us ... now.

How would we use these phrases? Here is an example.

Us: "I just found out how we can have energy all day long."

Prospect: "That sounds great! That is something I need."

Us: "Let's fix that now."

Prospect: "Uh, what do you mean?"

Us: "Take these super vitamin capsules twice a day. Let me know when you would like to start having more energy, and I will get it sorted."

Prospect: "Oh. Good idea."

When prospects want what we have, the conversation is fun.

Will every conversation be this easy? No.

There are many reasons why a prospect would not be interested in talking to us right now. Maybe:

- They are busy.
- They don't need what we have to offer.
- Their interests are elsewhere today.
- They are having a bad day.

Let's be polite. Allow our prospects an opportunity to say "no" and we save everyone time.

And that is it? Yes.

Short. Simple. Done.

Watch how easy
this can be.

Nam Do sells healthy coffee. As a network marketing professional, he has many great ice breakers. Here is just one. This is all he needs to say:

> "1. Do you drink coffee?

> "2. Would it be okay if your coffee made you healthier?

> "3. Let's order you some now."

Done.

Can't make that choice any easier for prospects.

But listen to this. Nam also says:

"Training new team members is easy. If they can memorize three sentences and take the volunteers, they can have a great part-time income."

What a great way to get new team members started. They can now earn money while learning the skills to be better in their business.

Another example?

> "1. Do you feel stressed?

> "2. Would it be okay if you could reduce your stress levels without smashing your dishes?"

Our prospects might smile and say, "Yeah! I want it now!"

Let's review.

Our conversation has a great ice breaker. It is not pushy. It easily introduces our business into a social conversation.

Then our ice breaker also closes our prospect with, "Would it be okay if ..."

No pressure. Just needs a "yes" or "no" answer.

If the answer is "yes," then we could put their decision into action by saying, "Let's fix that now."

Prospects prefer simple choices. They don't have time for reviewing complicated compensation plans, weighing ten different options, and reviewing industry data and statistics. Long presentations may interest a few people, but the majority want quick, clear choices. Then they can get on with their lives.

If prospects prefer simple, we should deliver simple. If they need more information in any one area, they will gladly ask.

Short is always better than long.

Want to add a bit more to this short conversation?

Try saying this:

• • •

"When you eat, do you normally eat junk food, or do you try to eat healthier when you can?"

"Then you will love this."

"Would you like to feel even better every day?"

"Would it be okay if you try this for 30 days and see how awesome you can feel?"

"Let's get that sorted now."

• • •

These five sentences won't take long to memorize.

Let's see what is happening sentence by sentence.

"When you eat, do you normally eat junk food, or do you try to eat healthier when you can?"

The first sentence commits our prospects to better health. Most prospects don't want poor health. Once prospects make a verbal commitment to better health, they want to be consistent. No one wants to later say, "No. I changed my mind. I want bad health."

Once our prospects make a commitment to better health, we win.

If we don't get this commitment, here is what can happen. At the end of our conversation, our prospects might say, "No. I don't think so. I am not that concerned about nutrition right now."

At the end of our first sentence, we should know if we will have a customer or not.

Here is what is even better. This sentence is totally non-invasive. Any new team member will feel comfortable asking this question several times a day!

What a great way to prospect for customers with no rejection.

"Then you will love this."

Here is what happens when we say, "Then you will love this." Our prospects take a positive frame of mind. In a way, we command them to love what we are going to say next. How good is that?

"Would you like to feel even better every day?"

Of course our prospects will say, "Yes." But think about this from our new team members' points of view. Getting "yes" responses from their prospects gives them confidence. When they feel good, it shows. People like doing business with people who are confident.

"Would it be okay if you try this for 30 days and see how awesome you can feel?"

Another "yes" answer from our prospects. Not only do our team members feel even more confident, they also close their prospect immediately. Their prospects have already committed to better health from the first question. No more stress. The decision has been made.

"Let's get that sorted now."

This moves the sale forward and puts everyone into action now. These words sound confident. Most prospects follow our suggestion to get healthier now.

Using proven phrases makes building our business quick and easy.

Network marketing professional Eugene Hong is a master of these short, proven phrases that get prospects to say "yes" quickly. In a few words, he gets his prospects interested, qualified, nodding, and closed. Eugene has plenty of phrases he can use to turn skeptics into fans, but that comes with time.

Compare his skill with brand-new distributors. They randomly talk and hope prospects figure things out for themselves. This is a bad plan. Prospects don't have time for us to be unprofessional.

We have to be like Eugene. Get to the point and make it clear, so prospects can say "yes" immediately.

Step #4:
Presentation.

Our prospects love what we've said so far and respond, "Sounds pretty good. But I need to know more."

Now is the time for our presentation. The decision has been made. Now it is a matter of details. But how many details?

Let's listen closely to exactly what our prospects said. They said, "I need to know more." They didn't say, "Please tell me everything you have ever learned about your business."

Time to be polite. We don't want to tell people more than they want to know. It is rude, a waste of their time, and might even talk them out of it. More people talk themselves out of a sale than listen their way out of a sale. It is better to say too little than to say too much. If we say too little, they can always ask for more.

In past years, salesmen believed that sales presentations convinced prospects to make decisions. There was a lot of pressure to create elaborate presentations with graphics, videos, PowerPoint, and endless proof and testimonials. Now, we know that was wrong. Decisions happen before the presentation begins.

We don't need a sales presentation to convince prospects to want what they already want. That means all the pressure is off us, and our prospects. Now our presentations can be a relaxed conversation where we answer our prospects' questions, and help them understand the details.

For some prospects, all they may want to know is the name of the company. For others, they may want to know every detail about our business. Not everyone will want the same amount of information. So how do we know how much information our prospects might want?

Here are some possibilities:

- Micro-presentation. Give a three- or four-sentence micro-presentation that summarizes the big picture. Then, wait for our prospects to ask for more details.

- Give a one-minute presentation. Then, wait for our prospects to ask for more details.

- Tell a two-minute story. Then, wait for our prospects to ask for more details.

- Ask an individual prospect, "What would you like to know first?" Then, continue answering questions as they arise.

Notice that none of the above options include, "Tell our prospects everything we know. Read the PowerPoint presentation to them as if they are reading-impaired. Bore prospects with one-size-fits-all corporate commercial videos. And tell prospects to quietly sit and save their questions until the end, while we talk **at** them about our wonderful company and products."

When we first start our business, we haven't learned a lot of presentation techniques. We don't know much about our business. Our confidence may not be at peak levels. In that case, we will default to a presentation that has a lower chance of success.

That would be sending our prospects away to look at a website or a corporate video. Then we hope our prospects will magically get excited, and come back to us begging to join. It could happen, but not often. But in the beginning, this might be our only option.

We can get better.

Why should we improve our skills? So that we can treat our prospects like people, not just numbers that we send away to watch a pre-packaged sales pitch. We want to honor our prospects as real people with real needs. This is the power of person-to-person network marketing.

If all it took was sending out millions of messages to watch a video, our companies wouldn't need us. They could do this themselves. Our person-to-person connections give us a huge advantage over corporate advertisements.

Which presentation do you think is more powerful?

1. Our mother sees an online ad to buy some vitamins. Or,

2. We personally ask our mother to buy our vitamins.

Which offer has more weight? The second one, of course. Big corporations would love to have the person-to-person advantage that we have.

As soon as possible, we need to learn some sort of effective presentation. So let's start with a small three- or four-sentence micro-presentation that gives our prospects the big picture. This might be all they need. Or if they would like to learn more, they can ask more questions based upon what we just presented.

Micro-presentations (the big picture).

This is an easy way to start.

Give a three- or four-sentence micro-presentation that summarizes the big picture for our prospects. Once they hear the big picture, they have some choices.

1. "That is all I need to know. Let's get started."

2. "Could you tell me a bit more?"

3. "I would like to see a long, formal presentation."

We follow the path our prospects want. Nothing complicated. They appreciate that we are there to help them.

Here is an example of a business opportunity micro-presentation if we sold health products.

"We don't sell. Everybody has already decided they want to be healthy and live longer. We just offer them a great product to help. Most want our product and we get paid."

That is a clear message. Our prospects "get it" without having to listen to a lot of fluff or hype.

Will our prospects appreciate this big-picture view? Yes! Because now we pause.

This pause allows prospects to ask for an additional explanation on anything we said. There is nothing worse than prospects having questions but no chance to ask them. That creates unnecessary tension in our prospects. We hate it when salespeople give a monologue with no pauses. We feel frustrated because we want to ask a question. We don't want to be one of those non-stop salespeople.

Let's look at this micro-presentation for our products.

> "People want to feel better. They love how this health drink makes them feel awesome. They love it so much, most tell their friends."

Now our prospects are thinking, "I should tell my friends to talk to you also. They feel tired and want to feel better too."

Big tip: It is easier to get referrals by including in the last sentence, "Most tell their friends."

Two more examples.

> "People can stress and worry about getting all the nutrition they need daily, or take our natural nutrition drink to guarantee it. This not only helps you sleep at night, but you will feel great also."

> "Keep your family healthy. Let your friends and neighbors do the same. Get a check every month for letting others benefit too."

Nothing scary about these presentations. And they don't take very long to learn.

Can we use this for our business opportunity?

Yes. The previous micro-presentations proved that our initial business opportunity presentation doesn't have to be complicated.

We don't have to explain every detail. All we do is give the big picture. Our prospects can decide which part of the big picture they want to know more about. Or, they could appreciate that our big picture got to the point, and they feel comfortable.

If we like, we can add a few extra sentences, but always keep our micro-presentations short. Here are some examples.

"You will feel great. Let your neighbors know that they can feel great also. They will love you. You get paid every time they order."

"Be a hero. Let your friends and neighbors know they can slow down the aging process by taking good care of their health. Get a paycheck for helping them."

"Want your own part-time business helping people be healthier? Feel good about making a difference. Build your business to a full-time income."

"Want a career helping people have a better life? Feel good every day when you help others live longer. The more people you help, the more you earn."

"Have big dreams? Build a business network of part-timers who help their friends and neighbors get healthier fast. The bigger your network, the bigger your paycheck."

"Everyone wants options on how to live healthier and longer. Keep giving more people the chance to choose, and you might be able to replace your full-time income. No more commuting."

Obviously these are abbreviated versions of our opportunity. This big-picture overview allows our prospects to relax and feel comfortable with what we offer. There will be plenty of time to talk about the company background and the finer details of the compensation plan after our prospect relaxes.

When we are clear about the big picture, skepticism goes away. We present the facts as an option for our prospects' lives. Our prospects can make their choices for their lives.

Will this short overview be enough for most prospects? Probably not. But it does relax them and help them figure out which questions they would like to ask. It is much better to be in a conversation than in a sales presentation.

Let's jump ahead and do a more structured short presentation.

The one-minute presentation.

Give a 30-minute presentation, and we will hear objections such as:

- "I need to think it over."
- "I couldn't do this. Memorizing this presentation would be impossible."
- "Can I get back to you later? I need to do something right now."
- "I don't have any time now. I can't take on another project."
- "I don't know anyone. I seldom go out."
- "Looks like you have to be a salesman. This is not for me."
- "I don't know how to do this. I wouldn't be any good at it."
- "My spouse and I don't do these sorts of things."

Are these real objections? No.

Our prospects are being polite and telling us "no" without rejecting us personally.

What went wrong? Our prospects couldn't see themselves talking to their friends and relatives like we did to them. This is a clue. We should present to our prospects in a way that feels more comfortable for them.

Getting more appointments.

The one-minute presentation makes it easy to get appointments. We don't have to call someone and ask them for 30 minutes or an hour of their time. Instead, we ask permission for a short one-minute presentation. For our prospects, it is easier for them to grant us permission than to try and avoid us.

All we need to do is memorize two sentences. Here they are:

1. "I can give you a complete presentation, but it would take an entire minute."

2. "When could you set aside a whole minute?"

What will most people will say?

"Go ahead. I am curious about this. Tell me now."

Our prospects will be listening. We will not be fighting through sales filters or salesman alarms. They will look forward to our one-minute explanation.

We could use these two sentences over the phone. Sometimes our prospects don't want to invest 30 minutes or an hour in a meeting. They want the big picture now. Why? Because they value their time.

To protect their time, they are looking for something they don't want. That means they can get out of the conversation right away. They won't have to invest their valuable time listening to details about something that is not a good fit for them.

When we deliver the big picture to these skeptical prospects, they feel good. Because we did not withhold information from them, they don't react with skepticism and resistance. Now they are more open-minded.

It gets better.

Our "big picture" is more structured in the one-minute presentation. We want to answer our prospects' three most pressing questions:

1. "What kind of business are you in?"

2. "How much money can I make?"

3. "Exactly what do I have to do to earn that money?"

It won't take long to answer these three questions.

If we answer these three questions clearly, our prospects can then tell us:

1. "Yes, I want to join."

2. "No, I don't want to join."

3. "I have a question or two."

Here is a quick generic example of a one-minute presentation that takes less than 15 seconds:

"You can become a stunt driver for movie productions. You can earn $100,000 a year. And all you have to do is risk your life daily by driving like a maniac."

Our prospects received the answers to their three basic questions:

1. "What kind of business are you in?" (You can become a stunt driver for movie productions.)

2. "How much money can I earn?" (You can earn $100,000 a year.)

3. "Exactly what do I have to do to earn that money?" (And all you have to do is risk your life daily by driving like a maniac.)

Clear, simple, and enough of a presentation that most people can make their decision.

Let's look at how we could answer these three questions for our health and nutrition business.

Question #1:
"What kind of business are you in?"

This is not a good time to be vague or to try and sound important. This is a great time to be clear and to the point. We want our prospects to understand.

Our prospects don't want to know the finer details of our business yet. They first want to know what kind of business it is. Why? Because no one would ever join a business if they didn't know what kind of business it was. Or maybe our prospect has a prejudice against certain types of businesses. Now is a good time to find out.

Here are some possible ways of answering that first question.

"We are in the health and nutrition business. Everyone wants to feel better and live longer."

"We are in the health business. People think about their health all the time."

This simple explanation lets our prospects know what we do. If we find that this explanation is not clear enough, we can add a bit more. The easiest transition words are "which means." Here is an example:

"We are in the nutrition business, which means when people can't eat healthy every meal, we step in and help."

The long explanation and details will be saved for only those prospects who are interested.

Question #2: "How much money can I make?"

This is a great place to use our common sense and listening skills. If our prospects do not give us a hint about how much money they want to earn, we could guess.

Or, to be more accurate, we could ask them.

Someone looking to change careers will want to know how to make a lot of money. Others may only want a part-time income to help with the family budget. How would this sound in real life?

To start off our one-minute presentation, we could say, "If you wanted to earn an extra $500 a month, you would have to do these three things."

Yes, we would start our one-minute presentation by immediately telling our prospects a monthly figure they could earn. No need to hold them in suspense. Prospects love us when we get to the point.

As we continue our one-minute presentation, our prospect can now focus on our explanation of our business. But at the end of our presentation, we will again remind our prospect of the monthly amount.

We could end by saying, "And then you would earn an extra $500 a month."

Don't worry about this now. We will give a complete one-minute presentation in a moment so we can see how everything fits in.

Question #3:
"Exactly what do I have to do to earn this money?"

This is where the magic happens. This is the burning question all prospects have.

Of course our answer to this question will depend on what our prospects want to earn. So, we will do a few examples.

All of these examples are approximations. At this point in the conversation, our prospects don't want to know every rule about qualifying for certain bonus levels. Our prospects don't want 10 different examples. What do they want? A rough overview of the activity they would have to do to earn this amount of money.

Here is what they don't want to hear:

"Just talk to people."

"Share our message with your friends."

These answers feel too vague. We will give them one example. Will this one example be 100% accurate 100% of the time? No. The purpose of this example is only to answer, "What do I have to do to earn this money?"

The key is to make this clear and short. Some examples:

"Spend two evenings a week helping people stop their bodies from rusting and aging. At the end of six months, you will be earning $500 extra a month."

"Every week, help one family get serious about their health. And out of all the people you help, eventually find four people who want a part-time income doing the same thing. At the end of one year, you will be earning an extra thousand dollars a month."

"Find four people who hate their jobs and want a bigger opportunity in their lives. Help each of them get their first 50 customers, and then you will be earning an extra $2000 a month."

Now, are any of these examples 100% accurate for your business? Of course not. They could be higher or lower depending on your compensation plan, fast-start bonuses, special promotions, if your new team members sponsored other team members, etc.

All of those comparisons can be made later in training. For now, our prospects only want to know, "Generally, what type of **activity** will I be doing to earn this money?" Let's be polite and answer this pressing question in their minds.

Let's put all three steps together.

Our prospects tell us, "Yes. I have one minute. Tell me about the business." Our answer?

"We are in the health and nutrition business. Everyone wants to live longer and feel younger. You can earn an extra $500 a month. All you have to do is spend two evenings a week helping families slow down their aging problem by putting better stuff in their bodies. At the end of six months, you will be earning an extra $500 a month."

Wow. That takes less than 20 seconds.

Is this everything our prospects want to know? No.

However, this is all they want to know right now. This gives them a chance to make an initial "yes" or "no" decision without investing a lot of their time. If this sounds interesting to them, we can explain all the details next.

In time, we will learn to do this more elegantly. But for now, this will be sufficient for most people that we will be talking to.

Notice what we left out.

We didn't talk about:

- How organic nutrition differs from synthetic vitamins.
- Our unique research patent.
- The background of our company's leader.
- The different steps in the compensation plan.
- Where we can set up the PowerPoint presentation.
- Our company's commercial videos.
- The size of the health and nutrition industry now.

In less than 20 seconds, our prospects have the big picture. If they don't like what they heard, they can say "no" right away and we will still be friends. We don't have to avoid each other in the future.

Our prospects can also say, "I think this is great. Sign me up."

And if our prospects want more details, they can ask. We will do our best to answer the questions as clearly as possible.

This one-minute presentation works face-to-face, on the phone, or on a video call. No more misleading invitations to secret meetings. Our prospects can relax by knowing what to expect.

Now, let's see how this one-minute presentation might sound in real life.

> **Us:** "I can give you a complete presentation, but it would take an entire minute. When could you set aside a whole minute?"

> **Prospect:** "Right now. Go ahead."

Our presentation:

> "If you want to earn an extra $500 a month, you would have to do these three things."

> (When we say three things, our prospects feel that we are getting directly to the point, no long sales pitch. And three things don't sound that intimidating either.)

> "Number one: Don't change. Continue recommending things you like." (Our prospects feel comfortable. It is natural for humans to recommend things we like to others. This also tells our prospects that they will stay within their comfort zones.)

> "Number two: We are in the health business. Everyone wants better health and longer lives. We simply spend a few minutes with them to show them how to put better health in their bodies." (Our prospects understand our business. This is clear.)

"And number three: All you have to do is spend two evenings a week showing people how to feel awesome by adding healthier products to their lives. At the end of six months, you will be earning $500 extra a month." (Our prospects know this will take two evenings away from television, and won't expect to earn $500 a month right away.)

Done!

Now we give our prospects a chance to speak. There is nothing worse than us talking too long. When we stop speaking, our prospects have a choice. We just wait for our prospects to make the choice that serves them best at this moment in their lives.

Some people fear change. They will insist on keeping their current lives exactly the same. That is okay. That makes them happy.

Other people welcome a change for better health and more money. They will insist on changing immediately. They feel every second wasted is money out of their pockets. We can help them change now.

When we visit with prospects, they have no obligation to buy or join. We simply offer our products or business as an option for their lives.

Let's do one more example.

"If you want to earn an extra $500 a month, you would have to do these three things.

"Number one: Don't change. Continue to recommend things that you like, such as your favorite music or favorite movie.

"Number two: We are in the health and wellness business, which means we help people stop their bodies from rusting from the inside out, so they look and feel younger naturally.

"Number three: All you have to do is help one person join your team every month, and help that person get their first four happy customers to kickstart their business.

"And then, at the end of eight months, you would earn an extra $500 a month."

When we are clear, our prospects relax and hear our message.

But what if our prospects don't make an immediate decision?

"Thinking it over" is the same as making a "no" decision. "Thinking it over" is a decision to not change. It is okay if our prospects consciously make a decision to stay where they are. We just want to make sure they are aware that "thinking it over" means they are turning down better health, or turning down the opportunity for more money in their lives.

Here is a simple closing statement that helps prospects understand that they will either make a decision to change, or make a decision to stay where they are. Here it is:

"This either works for you, or not. So what do you want to do?"

Some examples?

"Slowing down and getting older every day either works for you, or not. So what do you want to do?"

"Feeling young and great every day either works for you, or not. So what do you want to do?"

"Having an extra $500 a month in your family's budget either works for you, or not. So what do you want to do?"

"Building a part-time business in your spare time so that you can quit your job next year either works for you, or not. So what do you want to do?"

"Having a career where you can work out of your home instead of fighting traffic either works for you, or not. So what do you want to do?"

"Protecting your heart and circulation either works for you, or not. So what do you want to do?"

This basic closing statement helps prospects focus on what they want for their lives. When we ask this question, they don't feel pressured. Instead, they relax because now they know they are in charge of their choices for their lives.

Don't stress.

Our ice breaker pre-closed our prospects. The hard work of closing is already over. Our presentation is the easiest part.

Plus, if we keep our presentation short, our prospects will feel great. Our prospects believe that a bad one-minute presentation is always better than a perfect 30-minute presentation. Prospects prefer talking rather than listening to us anyway.

And here is an added bonus. This presentation is so short that our prospects think, "I can do this business. This explanation is so easy."

Can we improve our presentation skills from here? Of course.

If we are brand-new, these short presentations are a good place to start. They will give us confidence and prevent us from talking too long.

The One-Minute Presentation book takes this skill much deeper. But for now, this short presentation can get us started immediately.

In the next chapter, let's look at a more advanced presentation for our business opportunity.

The two-minute story.

This presentation works when we talk to an individual prospect, but it is not appropriate for a group meeting. Why? Because we will have a conversation with our prospect. We need to get feedback from our prospect so that we can customize this presentation to our prospect's needs.

It is not appropriate for selling our products. The story is about our opportunity.

And it is not appropriate for someone looking for a small part-time income. This story only works well for someone looking for a career change.

Yes, this story has limits. But it makes it easy for prospects to see themselves succeeding in a full-time network marketing career.

Margaret Millar once said, "Most conversations are simply monologues delivered in the presence of a witness." And that is the problem with standard presentations. All the communication is one-way. We end up preaching to our prospects.

The two-minute story changes this. Instead of giving a one-size-fits-all memorized presentation, we create a story in our prospects' minds configured to their current situations.

But let's get to work now on an actual two-minute story. It is easier to demonstrate than to explain.

The invitation.

How do you think our prospects would respond if we said the following?

"I've got a good story."

Most prospects would say, "Great, tell me the story." Why? Because humans love stories.

Whenever someone tells a story, our mind says, "Stop. Listen to the story. It may be important for our survival." Also, a story is more interesting than presentations and facts. We love movies and books because they tell stories.

Even children love stories. From the moment they can talk, they say, "Mommy, Daddy, tell me a story." Not only do we get our prospects' interest, we get their favorable interest. That is important. They will hear what we have to say.

Let's continue the invitation.

"I've got a good story. Takes about two minutes. Might make you a lot of money, might not. Do you want to hear it?"

What do you think our prospects will say? "Yes!"

Think about this from our prospects' points of view. What do they like about this invitation?

- "I've got a good story." Prospects love listening to stories.

- "Takes about two minutes." Prospects love listening to short stories, not long stories.

- "Might make you a lot of money, might not." The possibility of money? This sounds very interesting.

- "Do you want to hear it?" We give our prospects an option of opting into continuing the conversation. No pressure. They can volunteer.

This simple invitation to the "two-minute story" gets our prospects to volunteer to hear our short presentation.

Here it is again. This is something we should memorize word-for-word, and have it ready to say at any moment:

"I've got a good story. Takes about two minutes. Might make you a lot of money, might not. Do you want to hear it?"

What's next?

We will start our story with a question. This will help us personalize this story.

"Would it be okay if you never had to show up for work again?"

Our prospects think, "What would that look like to me? Could I stay home and read or work on my music? Maybe I could homeschool my children and be with them as they grow up? Will this be my chance to travel to the places I've always wanted to see? Let me imagine what it would feel like to sleep in late every morning."

Our prospects will create the perfect vision in their minds. At this moment our prospects create a dream of what their lives could be. If our prospects don't have dreams, there will be no motivation for them to start.

This is better than us guessing what our prospects' dreams could be. Some people want to travel. Others want to pursue their passions. We don't know. So instead of guessing, let's allow our prospects to create their perfect visions.

Here is our second sentence:

"So how much money would you need every month, just to cover the basic bills, so that you would never have to show up at work?"

Is this too personal? No. We didn't ask how much money they currently earn. In most societies that would be rude. Instead, we only wanted to know the minimum amount they would need to take care of their current bills. This will be the minimum amount they need to stop showing up for work every day.

Notice we did **not** ask how much money they would **like** to earn. That number could be huge. We want to keep the amount as low as possible. Then it is easier to show how our opportunity can help them reach this goal. Imagine this number as just enough to pay the bills and eat out a few times every month.

Now that we have this number, we're done with our information-collecting process. Let's see what our presentation looks like so far.

• • •

"I've got a good story. Takes about two minutes. Might make you a lot of money, might not. Want to hear it?"

"Would it be okay if you never had to go to work again?"

"So how much money would you need a month, just to cover the basic bills, so that you would never have to show up at work?"

• • •

Assuming is better than selling.

Instead of selling the benefits of our products, we will assume that we have awesome value for our prospects. When we assume with confidence, our prospects naturally believe us. Why else would we be so confident?

We are not technically selling our prospects on our products at this moment. We just want our prospects to know that others will buy and use our products. We want to establish that there is a market for what we have to offer. No one wants to join a business where no one will buy.

Here is the sentence that we will use:

"Well, you know how most people want to live longer and be healthier?"

When we start with "Well, you know how," our prospects begin nodding "yes" immediately. Then, we say a fact that our prospects will agree with. "Most people want to live longer" is a great fact to use. Who could argue with that?

What happens? At this moment our prospects agree that many people will be in the market for what we offer. We accomplish our mission.

But what if we sell diet products? This example is about general health products, but we could substitute anything.

Our next sentence will tell our prospects a little bit about our company. We can insert a small sales plug for our business here.

"There is a company called [our company] that shows people how to get healthier, without spending four hours at the gym every day."

Our prospects will assume that our company is good, and helps people get healthier in their busy lives. They should be thinking, "Everyone would want this."

Just a few sentences so far. Here they are.

• • •

"I've got a good story. Takes about two minutes. Might make you a lot of money, might not. Want to hear it?"

"Would it be okay if you never had to go to work again?"

"So how much money would you need a month, just to cover the basic bills, so that you would never have to show up at work?"

"Well, you know how most people want to live longer and be healthier?"

"There is a company called [our company] that shows people how to get healthier, without spending four hours at the gym every day."

• • •

So far, so good. Our prospects are nodding "yes" and are on our side. No tension. No selling. No pressure.

But back to our story.

We have the details out of the way. Our prospect knows what we do in our business. We also know how much money our prospect needs to cover his minimum expenses, so that he doesn't have to go to work.

Now, let's get back to the original question we asked: "Would it be okay if you never had to go to work again?" Our prospect might be wondering when are we going to tell him how he can stay home instead of going to work.

So, let's continue. We will say:

"Now, if you wanted to never go to work again, all you would have to do is help 400 families start buying better nutritional products instead of the generic stuff they normally buy."

Let's explain this sentence. We started our sentence by saying, "Now, if you wanted to never go to work again." We start with this phrase to refocus our prospect on the original question. We don't want our prospect thinking about something else at this time.

Then we say, "All you have to do is." This signals to our prospect that our explanation will be concise and easy to understand. Prospects love this.

And finally, we have to explain the compensation plan. At this point in the conversation, our prospect doesn't want to know the details of the compensation plan. Our prospect wants to know, "Generally, what would I have to do to earn this money so that I can stay home?"

Our prospect does not understand our network marketing terminology. We can't use words such as "legs" or "levels" or "group volume." We have to communicate our explanation in terms our prospect can understand immediately.

So how do prospects understand business? They visualize a shop with customers. They measure a business by its customers. So, we will use the customer explanation.

The last part of our sentence will be, "Help 400 families start buying better nutritional products instead of the generic stuff they normally buy."

This is clear and easy to understand for any prospect.

But there is a problem. Our prospect will panic and think, "400 families! I don't know 400 families. That is impossible!"

Don't worry. We will take care of this fear in the next sentence.

But how did we arrive at 400 families? It is an approximation. We know roughly how much is earned on each customer. But, it changes depending on if we found that customer personally, if our team found the customer, if there was some sort of fast-start bonus or promotion at that time, etc. Plus, we adjust the number of customers based upon how much income our prospect needs to stay home and cover his bills. Someone who needs $5000 a month will need a lot more customers.

Don't worry about the exact number. We just want to pick something close so that our prospect understands our business.

Overcoming our prospect's panic attack.

Our prospect thinks, "400 customers! That is too many. I could never do that."

To relax our prospect, we will do a mind-reading trick. Yes, we will read our prospect's mind. We will say:

"Now, you don't know how to get 400 customers, but you can learn. You learned how to use a smartphone, you learned how to use that 100-button remote control for your television, and you certainly can learn a system to help 400 customers get healthier and happier."

Wow! Now what is our prospect thinking?

"Oh, you are so right. I don't know how to get 400 customers. You read my mind. I can trust you. And I did learn how to use my smartphone. And that remote control? That was tough, but I learned. I could be a borderline genius. I have the ability to learn new things. Now, they say they have a system. I like how that sounds. I can get step-by-step instructions that I can learn and follow. While this sounds difficult now, their system will train me to get 400 customers. So, I think I can learn their system and do this."

This one sentence does a lot of work. At the end of the sentence, our prospect sees the possibility of our business replacing his full-time income at work.

Won't this sentence bring up a lot of questions from our prospect?

Possibly. Some prospects can have lots of questions.

The good news is that we don't have to be experts to answer these questions. Most of the questions can be answered by saying, "You will learn how to do that when you learn our system."

Here are some examples.

Prospects: "I don't know where to find people who want to get healthier or live longer."

Us: "Don't worry. You will learn how to do that when you learn our system."

Prospects: "I don't know how to talk to people."

Us: "Don't worry. You will learn how to talk to people when you learn our system."

Prospects: "I am a shy person. I am not comfortable talking to strangers."

Us: "Don't worry. You will learn how to be very comfortable with others when you learn our system."

Prospects: "I don't know how to do this or any business."

Us: "Don't worry. The company doesn't expect us to know how to do this business before we start. That is why we have training. You will learn how to do this business step-by-step when you learn our system."

We will answer our prospects' questions by referring to the "system." This will give our prospects confidence that they can successfully build their business.

Before we explain all the details of our system, we first need to get a decision from our prospect. There is no need to go through all the details of our training with someone if they are not going to join. That would waste a lot of time.

But, before we close, let's see how our two-minute story looks so far.

• • •

"I've got a good story. Takes about two minutes. Might make you a lot of money, might not. Want to hear it?"

"Would it be okay if you never had to go to work again?"

"So how much money would you need a month, just to cover the basic bills, so that you would never have to show up at work?"

"Well, you know how most people want to live longer and be healthier?"

"There is a company called [our company] that shows people how to get healthier, without spending four hours at the gym every day."

"Now, if you wanted to never go to work again, all you would have to do is help 400 families start buying better nutritional products instead of the generic stuff they normally buy."

"Now, you don't know how to get 400 customers, but you can learn. You learned how to use a smartphone, you learned how to use that 100-button remote control for your television, and you certainly can learn a system to help 400 customers get healthier and happier."

• • •

Our "two-minute story" is looking great! So let's get the "yes" or "no" decision from our prospect.

How to wrap it up and get the decision.

To do this, we will ask a simple question. We want to know if our prospect wants to stay where he is, keep his life the same … or if our prospect wants to go into business with us.

That is it. That is the only decision we need at this point.

If our prospect gives us a "no" decision, and prefers to keep his life the same, that is okay. We are done. Our prospect will still remember this story. So when times are difficult in the future, our prospect will think of us, and think of us fondly. Timing is everything.

How do we ask this closing question? Here it is.

"So what is going to be easier for you?"

What a nice question. No pressure on our prospect. We look great also. We don't look like some sleazy salesman with an agenda. All we do is ask our prospect if he wishes to keep his life the same, or join our business. We leave our prospect in control of his life.

How do we do this? We continue our question with two choices.

Choice #1: Keep your life as it is. Don't change anything.

Choice #2: Change your life. Start your new business now.

Here are some examples.

"So what is going to be easier for you? To continue struggling with one paycheck? Or to start learning a system for your new business so that you never have to show up for work again?"

"So what is going to be easier for you? To continue waking up at 6 AM every morning to fight traffic to work? Or, to learn a system so that you can have your own business and work out of your home?"

"So what is going to be easier for you? To continue going to the job you hate five days a week? Or to start your business with us tonight, so maybe next year you can work out of your home?"

"So what is going to be easier for you? To continue letting other people raise your children at daycare? Or to start your business this evening so that maybe next year you can be home with the children?" (Okay, a bit strong. But it is easy to remember.)

"So what is going to be easier for you? To hope for a 50% pay raise at work? Or, to enroll in training now and learn the system, so that you never have to show up at work again?"

"So what is going to be easier for you? To work two jobs for the rest of your life to make ends meet? Or to start tonight, create a part-time business to help with monthly expenses, and build it to a full-time business quickly?"

And then we are done.

Our prospects can choose which option will be easier for them. They choose the option, and we have no need for closing. We respect our prospect's choice.

Let's take a look at this two-minute story in its entirety.

The whole story.

Ready?

This is the story that can change our lives.

• • •

"I've got a good story. Takes about two minutes. Might make you a lot of money, might not. Want to hear it?"

"Would it be okay if you never had to go to work again?"

"So how much money would you need a month, just to cover the basic bills, so that you would never have to show up at work?"

"Well, you know how most people want to live longer and be healthier?"

"There is a company called [our company] that shows people how to get healthier, without spending four hours at the gym every day."

"Now, if you wanted to never go to work again, all you would have to do is help 400 families start buying better nutritional products instead of the generic stuff they normally buy."

"Now, you don't know how to get 400 customers, but you can learn. You learned how to use a smartphone, you learned how to use that 100-button remote control for your television, and you certainly can learn a system to help 400 customers get healthier and happier."

"So what is going to be easier for you? To continue going to the job you hate five days a week? Or to start your business with us tonight, so maybe next year you can work out of your home?"

• • •

If this story could make us financially free, how much effort should we put into learning it?

Yes, it is a bit more complicated than a four- or five-sentence presentation, but it is worth it.

And if this story could make presenting effortless for us and our prospects, how often would we use it? It certainly makes phone conversations shorter.

Ask network marketing professional Dale Moreau, who is one of the best at using the two-minute story to build his business. Everything we need to do is over in less than two minutes. No more long initial presentations only to find out our prospects aren't interested.

Prospects love the two-minute story. Think about this from their viewpoint. It is all about them, and it is short and to the point.

Once we tell the story for a few weeks, we can repeat this story in our sleep. Instead of worrying what comes next in the story, we can then focus on our prospects and how we can help them.

The two-minute story is the most powerful business opportunity presentation we can give one-on-one with a prospect. We customize the story to our prospect's income needs. The story is all about our prospect. It is the most interesting story in the world.

Can this two-minute story get better? Sure. *The Two-Minute Story* book takes this presentation skill to a higher level, but we don't have to learn that now. We can start with any of the presentations we have learned so far in this book. The key is to start. Taking action is better than perfecting skills that we never use with prospects.

Group presentations.

Ever feel nervous in front of a group?

Relax. This is normal. Why do we feel nervous?

Because the entire group is judging us. That would make anyone nervous!

When we stand up in front of a group, here is what others are thinking. "Who are you? Will you be interesting? Is this going to be a sales pitch? How long is this going to last? Should I believe you? Let me evaluate your sense of fashion."

Our group is not thinking about our business opportunity. They are too busy judging us.

Take control of their minds immediately.

Humans can have only one thought at a time. Let's put another thought in their minds so they won't have room for all these negative thoughts about us. How will we engage their minds?

We can start with a question. Now the group has to think about their answers to our question. Their minds are off of us, and on to answering the question. Problem solved.

After our initial question, we can continue challenging their minds. That way they will focus on what we're presenting to them.

And here is the good news.

We only have to control their minds for the first 30 seconds. After 30 seconds, our group will make their decisions. So we want to get our entire message compressed into the first 30 seconds. Anyone can learn and memorize 30 seconds' worth of information about their business. Want to see this in action?

We will come to the front of the group, and say this.

• • •

"Here is the short story. How many people here this evening want to be healthier and live longer? Ask yourself, 'Would it be okay if I knew how to slow down my aging and feel younger?' That is what we do. Now, ask yourself, 'Would my neighbors love me more if I allowed them to feel better too?' Of course they will. By doing this, you will earn money every time your neighbors use our products."

• • •

Notice that we did not talk **at** our prospects. We had a conversation with them. A pleasant conversation.

Our conversation was so engaging, our prospects didn't have time to think about us or judge us. Did you notice how we kept our prospects' minds engaged?

This entire opening to our group presentation took only 30 seconds. Most prospects will be thinking at the end of our 30 seconds, "Yeah. This makes sense. Sounds pretty good to me."

At this point, our prospects are on our side. Now they welcome the details we are about to show them. Prospects will want details only after they make a "yes" decision.

Let's see why this works so well. We will analyze each sentence.

"Here is the short story." (This opening sentence relaxes our prospects. It announces to them that we will get to the point, and not waste their time with some boring, long-winded presentation.)

"How many people here this evening want to be healthier and live longer?" (Our prospects now consider this question in their minds. They think, "Sure. I never thought dying early was a good plan." And now they forget about us. They are thinking about themselves and their health.)

"Ask yourself, 'Would it be okay if I knew how to slow down my aging and feel younger?'" (We have our prospects talking to themselves about our business. This question is a no-brainer. We know our prospects will say "yes" to this question.)

"That is what we do." (Clear and to the point. Our prospects love what we do. How good is that?)

"Now, ask yourself, 'Would my neighbors love me more if I allowed them to feel better too?'" (Their minds picture their neighbors. No time to be thinking about us.)

"Of course they will." (They can visualize themselves being thanked by their neighbors.)

"By doing this, you will earn money every time your neighbors use our products."

(Nothing else to discuss. We told the whole story in 30 seconds.)

Our first 30 seconds handled the decision. Everything past this point will be small details. We can relax.

We are only 30 seconds away from having a great group presentation about our business opportunity. It is what we say first that will make the difference. This is why we concentrate so hard on the first 30 seconds.

After this 30-second opening, we can cover the details in our presentation.

But what about a group presentation for potential customers?

Here is a different approach. We can start with our personal story, and our potential customers will see themselves in the same situation. They will visualize our story in their minds, but with themselves as the main characters. And guess what? They will come to the same conclusion that we did.

Here is an example of our story to start the group presentation.

"Growing old really hurts. Every morning when I woke up, I felt my age. Well, I decided that spending the rest of my life with no energy wasn't how I wanted to live. Now was the time to rebuild my body and start feeling younger. I started with this nutrition set. My body need better building materials. In 14 days, I started waking up feeling like a kid on Saturday mornings. I wish I'd started this 10 years ago."

Then we ask the group, "How do you feel when you wake up every morning?"

Our prospects will naturally make the same decision that we did. Feeling young and energetic is better than feeling old and tired.

But what if we don't personally use the product we represent? In that case, we will have to tell the audience someone else's story. For example, we could say, "My grandmother used to sit at home, complaining all day long. Never stopped. Everything was painful and she loved to tell us about it. Well, we got Grandma on this basic nutrition set, and now she is taking karate classes and breakdancing on weekends. I don't know what is in this stuff, but I am starting on it now."

Okay, a bit exaggerated, but we get the idea.

Group presentations are fun and easy to do. When we make the first 30 seconds awesome, the rest of the presentation is easy.

Where and how to find prospects.

We now have the skills to give short presentations. With a question or two, we can qualify our prospects. A few sentences are all we need to get our prospects to make "yes" decisions.

The good news is that our friends and relatives will enjoy our non-sales approach.

The bad news is that we will run out of people that we know quickly.

Where do we go from here? How do we find new prospects? Let's go to work.

Prejudging.

It sounds like a bad word, but it is something we do.

Not everyone is a prospect. People who live in the Amazon? Not prospects. People who are ill-tempered and hard to talk to? Not prospects. People younger than 18? Not prospects. As we can see, not everyone is a prospect for our business.

But, there are a lot of people left. Too many people for us to talk to. Our time is limited. So who should we choose to talk to? People who are open-minded and looking for what we have to offer? Or people who are too difficult or barely qualified?

The answer is obvious. If we can only talk to one segment of this large group, let's talk to the most qualified people. We want to talk to those that have the best chance of becoming customers or business partners.

Imagine this. Every person knows at least 200 people that we don't. We don't want to talk to all 200 people. Many fail to qualify. But out of the 200 people someone knows, there must be five or ten people who would be perfect for our business and our products. Let's spend our time talking to these prospects.

How do we find them? Ask.

We can ask our current customers. We can ask our friends who did not join. And we can ask complete strangers if they know people who want what we have to offer.

Here is the wrong way to ask for these referrals: "Do you know anyone that would be interested?" Most people will reply, "No." We won't get many referrals this way.

How can we ask for referrals in a rejection-free way? We will use this little script instead:

"I am curious. Can you do me a favor? I am looking for people with this problem, who want to fix it. Do you know anyone like that?"

This script will give us a better chance for referrals. Let's break this down sentence by sentence.

- "I am curious." There is something about this phrase that disarms people. It even makes mean people nice. These are great words to start a conversation with a stranger.

- "Can you do me a favor?" Most people are glad to do us a favor if it does not cost them money or obligate them to move our furniture.

- "I am looking for people with this problem, who want to fix it." We tell them the type of person we are looking for. This person has a problem. But we also qualify this by making sure they want to fix their problem. No use talking to them if they don't want to fix their problem.

- "Do you know anyone like that?" If we seem trustworthy, they will give us the name of someone who needs our help.

So what is "this problem" in this little script? It is a problem that we can solve. Let's see this in action.

"I am just curious. Could you do me a favor? I am looking for tired people who find it hard to wake up every morning. Do you know anyone like that?"

What was the problem? Waking up and starting our day when we are tired is a problem. Now we will get a referral of someone who wants to wake up every morning full of energy and excitement. This will be an easy person for us to talk to.

How about this?

"I am just curious. Could you do me a favor? I am looking for grandmothers who want so much energy that their grandchildren will whine, 'Grandma! Grandma! Slow down. We can't keep up!' Do you know anyone like that?"

This is the key sentence. "I am looking for people with this problem, who want to fix it." All we need to do is change this sentence in this little script, and we can have all the referrals we need.

Some examples of this key sentence for our business opportunity?

- I am looking for stressed single moms, who want to change their lives.
- I am looking for people with jobs, who want to be free.
- I am looking for college students with debt, who want a way to pay off their loans quickly.
- I am looking for people who are tired of commuting, and would rather work out of their homes.
- I am looking for people about to retire, who want to double their pension.
- I am looking for people with lots of credit card debt, who want a way of paying it off quickly.
- I am looking for people with low-paying careers who would like to earn a lot more.
- I am looking for people who like to travel, but would like to win free trips instead of spending their own money.
- I am looking for parents with jobs, who want more flexible hours so that they can be home with the children.
- I am looking for people who love coffee breaks and chatting with people, and would love to have a career taking five coffee breaks a day.

In 15 minutes, we could create a huge list of possible things we could say.

Here is my favorite one.

"I am looking for people with two jobs, who would like to get rid of one of those jobs."

What do we know about people with two jobs? Well, they need extra money. They are self-starters. They went out and got that extra job. Do they want to work two jobs for the rest of their lives? Of course not. If we could help them get rid of one of their jobs, they would be thrilled. We could expect a big hug. And if we could help them get rid of both of their jobs, they might hug us so hard it would crush our ribs.

This little prospecting script can point us towards the best, most open-minded prospects who other people know. So if we have a choice of who to talk to, let's talk to the most qualified people we can.

Finding good prospects to talk to is easy. So many people have problems, and we have solutions.

What to say at networking events.

Business breakfast clubs, local Chamber of Commerce mixers, lead-swapping groups, MeetUp groups, and more. There is no shortage of places where prospects get together. Here is an excerpt from our book, *51 Ways and Places to Sponsor New Distributors.*

• • •

Many years ago, Bob and Anna Bassett from Canada shared their "Five-Question Test." They told me the story of their friend, Herbie.

Herbie would be talking to a prospect at a networking event, and then suddenly, turn and walk away, sometimes in mid-sentence. When asked about the abrupt behavior, Herbie answered,

"Well, he didn't pass the Five-Question Test."

What's the Five-Question Test?

Herbie explained, "Well, when I meet somebody new, I try to learn as much as I can about him by asking questions. I ask him five questions during our conversation, and if he hasn't asked me anything, then I know he is only interested in himself. I just walk away. There is no point in talking to anyone who doesn't pass the Five-Question Test."

Prospecting isn't all about you. It is all about the prospects.

Don't start by talking all about you and your company. Soon no one will be listening. Instead, learn as much as you can about your prospects.

Find out if they have a problem you can solve. Build a relationship with them. Then, when they decide to solve their problem, they will choose to solve it with you.

It doesn't matter if your prospects pass the Five-Question Test. What matters is that **you** pass the Five-Question Test.

• • •

So how do we find out if our prospect has a problem? We ask.

Prospects love to talk. They will have no problem answering our questions.

Now, our prospect will be doing most of the talking. We listen. We pick up hints about our prospect's problems. When we hear a problem that we can solve, we will ask a question or make a comment about that problem. Sometimes we have to wait a bit before we get a chance to ask or comment.

Here are some examples of what our part of the conversation might sound like.

- "Are you okay with being so busy you don't have time for your family?"

- "How do you feel during that long commute every day?"

- "Do you expect a huge raise at work this year?"

- "Yeah. Jobs don't give us any hope. If we don't start our own business, then we are sentenced to a lifetime of labor."

- "You are right. Things are so expensive now. What are you doing to have more money come in every month?"

- "Yeah. It is impossible to get by on one paycheck now."

We could use this same technique at parties.

If we don't like to go to outside networking events, we can go to parties!

Help the host. Grab a tray of appetizers, and go guest-to-guest, offering them something to eat. What an easy way to start the conversation. It won't take us long to find an appropriate time to use our ice breaker.

How many parties can we go to? Oh my! This could be a fun challenge.

With unlimited pre-sold prospects to choose from, prospecting won't be a problem.

And finally.

All the techniques in this book work better when we use them. Having knowledge and not using it is the same as not having the knowledge.

So let's review the big picture.

Most prospects we meet are pre-sold. They want to be healthier. They want to live longer. They want more money in their lives.

We should talk to prospects in these four steps, keeping them in the correct order.

1. Build some rapport first.

2. Introduce our business with an ice breaker.

3. Close our prospects. Get their decision now.

4. And finally, if our prospects' answer is "yes," give them a presentation.

If we keep these steps in the correct order, we won't have to worry about rejection. Our prospects will love us.

And this makes our network marketing business not only fun, but profitable.

And as top network marketing leader Eugene Hong once said, "We want to be so successful in our own business, that every day we wake up when we are done sleeping."

Thank you.

Thank you for purchasing and reading this book. We hope you found some ideas that will work for you.

Before you go, would it be okay if we asked a small favor? Would you take just one minute and leave a sentence or two reviewing this book online? Your review can help others choose what they will read next. It would be greatly appreciated by many fellow readers.

More Big Al Books
BigAlBooks.com

Core Skills

How To Get Instant Trust, Belief, Influence and Rapport!
13 Ways To Create Open Minds By Talking To The Subconscious Mind

Learn how the pros get instant rapport and cooperation with even the coldest prospects. The #1 skill every new distributor needs.

Ice Breakers!
How To Get Any Prospect To Beg You For A Presentation

Create unlimited Ice Breakers on-demand. Your distributors will no longer be afraid of prospecting, instead, they will love prospecting.

Pre-Closing for Network Marketing
"Yes" Decisions Before The Presentation

Instead of selling to customers with facts, features and benefits, let's talk to prospects in a way they like. We can now get that "yes" decision first, so the rest of our presentation will be easy.

The Two-Minute Story for Network Marketing
Create the Big-Picture Story That Sticks!

Worried about presenting your business opportunity to prospects? Here is the solution. The two-minute story is the ultimate presentation to network marketing prospects.

Leadership Series

The Complete Three-Book Network Marketing Leadership Series
Series includes: How To Build Network Marketing Leaders Volume One, How To Build Network Marketing Leaders Volume Two, and Motivation. Action. Results.

Motivation. Action. Results.
How Network Marketing Leaders Move Their Teams

Learn the motivational values and triggers our team members have, and learn to use them wisely. By balancing internal motivation and external motivation methods, we can be more effective motivators.

How To Build Network Marketing Leaders
Volume One: Step-By-Step Creation Of MLM Professionals

This book will give you the step-by-step activities to actually create leaders.

How To Build Network Marketing Leaders
Volume Two: Activities And Lessons For MLM Leaders

You will find many ways to change people's viewpoints, to change their beliefs, and to reprogram their actions.

Personality Training

The Four Color Personalities for MLM
The Secret Language for Network Marketing

Learn the skill to quickly recognize the four personalities and how to use magic words to translate your message.

Mini-Scripts for the Four Color Personalities
How to Talk to our Network Marketing Prospects

As network marketing leaders, we want to move people to take positive actions. Using their own color language is how we will do it.

Why Are My Goals Not Working?
Color Personalities for Network Marketing Success

Setting goals that work for us is easy when we have guidelines and a checklist.

How To Get Kids To Say Yes!
Using the Secret Four Color Languages to Get Kids to Listen

Turn discipline and frustration into instant cooperation. Kids love to say "yes" when they hear their own color-coded language.

More Books

Why You Need to Start Network Marketing
How to Remove Risk and Have a Better Life

Discover the real reason why people are adding network marketing to their lives.

How To Build Your Network Marketing Utilities Business Fast

The complete starter manual for a successful network marketing business with utilities and services.

10 Shortcuts Into Our Prospects' Minds
Get network marketing decisions fast!

We only have a few seconds before our prospects make their decisions. Use these seconds wisely.

How to Get Your Prospect's Attention and Keep It!
Magic Phrases for Network Marketing

Getting attention is the easy part. Keeping that attention requires using these magic phrases to ward off distractions.

Quick Start Guide for Network Marketing
Get Started FAST, Rejection-FREE!

Our new team members are at the peak of their enthusiasm now. Let's give them the fast-start skills to kick-start their business immediately.

Create Influence
10 Ways to Impress and Guide Others

With ten unique strategies to choose from, we can change how the world reacts to us. Our voices will be heard. Our influence will create action.

How to Meet New People Guidebook
Overcome Fear and Connect Now

Meeting new people is easy when we can read their minds. Discover how strangers automatically size us up in seconds, using three basic standards.

How to Build Your Network Marketing Business in 15 Minutes a Day

Anyone can set aside 15 minutes a day to start building their financial freedom. Of course we would like to have more time, but in just 15 minutes we can change our lives forever.

Closing for Network Marketing
Getting Prospects Across The Finish Line

Here are 46 years' worth of our best closes. All of these closes are kind and comfortable for prospects, and rejection-free for us.

The One-Minute Presentation
Explain Your Network Marketing Business Like A Pro

Learn to make your business grow with this efficient, focused business presentation technique.

How to Follow Up With Your Network Marketing Prospects
Turn Not Now Into Right Now!

Don't lose all those prospects that didn't join on your first contact. Help reassure them that you and your opportunity can make a difference in their lives.

Retail Sales for Network Marketers
How to Get New Customers for Your MLM Business

Learn how to position your retail sales so people are happy to buy. Don't know where to find customers for your products and services? Learn how to market to people who want what you offer.

Getting "Yes" Decisions
What insurance agents and financial advisors can say to clients

In the new world of instant decisions, we need to master the words and phrases to successfully move our potential clients to lifelong clients.

3 Easy Habits For Network Marketing
Automate Your MLM Success

Use these habits to create a powerful stream of activity in your network marketing business.

Start SuperNetworking!
5 Simple Steps to Creating Your Own Personal Networking Group

Start your own personal networking group and have new, pre-sold customers and prospects come to you.

First Sentences for Network Marketing
How To Quickly Get Prospects On Your Side

Attract more prospects and give more presentations with great first sentences that work.

51 Ways and Places to Sponsor New Distributors
Discover Hot Prospects For Your Network Marketing Business

Learn the best places to find motivated people to build your team and your customer base.

How To Prospect, Sell And Build Your Network Marketing Business With Stories

If you want to communicate effectively, add your stories to deliver your message.

26 Instant Marketing Ideas To Build Your Network Marketing Business

176 pages of amazing marketing lessons and case studies to get more prospects for your business immediately.

Big Al's MLM Sponsoring Magic
How To Build A Network Marketing Team Quickly

This book shows the beginner exactly what to do, exactly what to say, and does it through the eyes of a brand-new distributor.

Public Speaking Magic
Success and Confidence in the First 20 Seconds

By using any of the three major openings in this book, we can confidently start our speeches and presentations without fear.

Worthless Sponsor Jokes
Network Marketing Humor

Here is a collection of worthless sponsor jokes from 25 years of the "Big Al Report." Network marketing can be enjoyable, and we can have fun making jokes along the way.

About the Authors

Keith Schreiter has 20+ years of experience in network marketing and MLM. He shows network marketers how to use simple systems to build a stable and growing business.

So, do you need more prospects? Do you need your prospects to commit instead of stalling? Want to know how to engage and keep your group active? If these are the types of skills you would like to master, you will enjoy his "how-to" style.

Keith speaks and trains in the U.S., Canada, and Europe.

Tom "Big Al" Schreiter has 40+ years of experience in network marketing and MLM. As the author of the original "Big Al" training books in the late '70s, he has continued to speak in over 80 countries on using the exact words and phrases to get prospects to open up their minds and say "YES."

His passion is marketing ideas, marketing campaigns, and how to speak to the subconscious mind in simplified, practical ways. He is always looking for case studies of incredible marketing campaigns that give usable lessons.

As the author of numerous audio trainings, Tom is a favorite speaker at company conventions and regional events.

Made in the USA
Coppell, TX
22 October 2020